Dirty
Thought
that Counts!

THIS IS A CARLTON BOOK

Published in 2012 by Carlton Books Limited
20 Mortimer Street
London W1T 3JW

10 9 8 7 6 5 4 3 2 1

Illustrations and design © Carlton Books Limited 2012
Text © Carlton Books Limited 2000, 2001, 2003, 2005

Some of the material in this book has previously appeared
in *The Biggest Book of Bloke Jokes Ever* (Carlton, 2004) and
The Best Dirty Girl's Joke Book Ever (Carlton © 2005).

A CIP catalogue record for this book is available from the
British Library.

ISBN 978 1 78097 230 5

Senior Executive Editor: *Lisa Dyer*
Managing Art Director: *Lucy Coley*
Editor: *Nicky Gyopari*
Design: *Barbara Zuñiga*
Production Manager: *Maria Petalidou*
Illustrations: *Katherine Asher*

Printed and bound by
CPI Group (UK) Ltd, Croydon, CR0 4YY

It's the
Dirty
Thought
that Counts!

Sexy Jokes for Saucy Girls

Karen S. Smith

CARLTON
BOOKS

Contents

1 *Jokes About Blokes*

Why are blokes like chocolate bars?
They're sweet, smooth and they usually head
right for your hips.

Why are blokes like laxatives?

They both irritate the shit out of you.

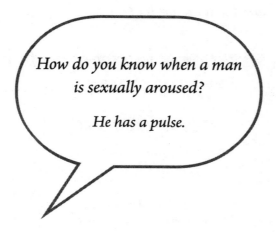

How do you know when a man
is sexually aroused?

He has a pulse.

How do you know when your bloke is getting old?

**When he starts having
dry dreams and wet farts.**

What's the difference between a man and a motorbike?

1. You can tell how big the exhaust pipe is before you start riding it.

2. You can swap motorbikes with your friend to see which is the better ride.

3. It's the motorbike that suffers if you don't use enough lubrication.

4. A motorbike stays between your legs till you've had enough fun.

5. You only chain a motorbike up when you've finished riding it.

Why does a penis have a hole in the end?

So blokes can be open-minded.

Why do men close
their eyes during sex?
They can't stand to see
a woman enjoying herself.

What's the difference between
a man and a condom?
Condoms aren't
thick and insensitive
these days.

What's the thickest book in the world?

What Blokes Think They Know about Women

Why are men like cowpats?

The older they get, the easier they are to pick up.

*How does a bloke keep a woman
screaming after climax?*

He wipes his willy on the curtains!

*What do you call a beautiful woman
on the arm of an ugly man?
A tattoo.*

Why is a bicycle better than a man?

1. You can ride your bicycle for as long as
you like, and it won't get there before you do.

2. A bicycle never complains at having
to wear rubber tyres.

3. You don't have to shave your legs
before you go out on your bicycle.

4. Your parents won't go on about how much
they liked your old bicycle.

5. Nothing goes soft on a bicycle that
a bicycle pump won't fix.

What's the difference between a man and a Rubik's cube?

No matter how long you play with a Rubik's cube, it'll still be hard.

What's the difference between a clitoris and a golf ball?

Men will spend hours looking for a golf ball.

Why are dogs better than men?

1. If a dog wants to go out, it will let you know.

2. A dog will express affection in public.

3. A dog will play ball without telling you how to throw overarm.

4. You can train a dog to understand what 'no' means.

5. *If a dog wants its balls licked, it will do it for itself.*

6. *After six months, a dog will still look excited to see you.*

7. *Just because you've had some fun with a dog, it doesn't think it can sleep on your bed.*

8. *Dogs feel guilt.*

9. *Dogs are grateful when you stroke them.*

10. *When your dog gets old, you can just get a younger dog.*

**What's the difference between
men and concrete?**

*Both take ages to get hard, but concrete
only has to be laid once.*

Why do blokes have their best ideas during sex?

Because they're plugged into a genius.

Why are blokes like fine wine?
They all start out like grapes, and it's our job to stomp on
them and keep them in the dark until they mature into
something you'd like to have dinner with.

What's the difference
between a beer and a man?
The beer comes in a can,
not in your mouth.

Why are blokes like floor tiles?
Lay them right the first time,
and you can walk all over them
for the rest of your life!

Why do bald men have holes in their pockets?

So they can run their fingers through their hair.

Why do women rub their eyes in the morning?

Because they haven't got balls.

Two women are discussing their blokes over coffee one day.

'You know,' says the first, 'my bloke eats like a pig,

drinks like a fish and is a rat as well.

In fact he makes me so sick I can barely eat.'

'Well, why don't you chuck him?' says the other woman.

'Well,' says the first. 'I just want to lose another 10 kilos…'

Why is a woman like a TV remote control?
Because a man will just sit there pushing buttons
randomly till something happens.

Why is a man like a dining table?
They both have an extra bit that
extends for entertaining.

Why are blokes like used cars?
Both are easy to get, cheap and unreliable.

Why are blokes like holidays?
They never seem to be long enough.

Why are blokes like lava lamps?
Fun to look at but not all that bright.

Why are blokes like popcorn?
They satisfy you,
but only for a little while.

Why are blokes like cement?
After getting laid,
they take a long time to get hard.

Why are blokes like cashpoint machines?
Once they withdraw, they lose interest.

Why are blokes like sperm?
They both have only a one in a million
chance of becoming a human being.

Why are blokes like tights?
They either cling, run or don't fit right in the crotch.

Why is a bloke like a computer?

You don't realize how much either of them

means to you until they go down on you.

Why are blokes like a snowstorm?
'Cos you don't know when they're coming,
how long they're going to last
or how many inches you'll get.

> *If you have an intelligent woman, an intelligent bloke and Santa Claus in a lift, which is the odd one out? The intelligent woman – because the other two don't exist.*

What's the difference between women's relationships with their children and blokes'?

Women know about their children's dentist appointments, football games, romances, best friends, favourite foods, secret fears and dreams. Blokes are vaguely aware of some short people living in the house.

What's a bloke's idea of foreplay? **Watching the end of the match first.**

What do blokes use for birth control? **Their personality.**

What's the best form of birth control for a bloke over 50? **Nudity.**

What do you call the insensitive bit at the base of a penis? **A bloke.**

What do you call a bloke who says he's in touch with his feminine side? **A liar.**

What happens when a vain and irritating bloke takes Viagra? **He gets taller.**

What do you call a bloke with a big willy and lots of cash? **Darling.**

What do you call a bloke with an IQ of five? **Gifted.**

What does the smart bloke do in an M&M factory? **Proofread.**

How can you tell if a bloke is excited?
He's breathing.

How can you grow your own dope?
Bury a bloke
and wait for spring.

How many divorced blokes
does it take to change a lightbulb?
Nobody knows, they never get the house!

How can a bloke tell when a woman
has had a good orgasm?

When the buzzing of her
vibrator stops.

How do blokes exercise on the beach?
By sucking in their stomach every time a bikini goes by.

How can you tell the
difference between
blokes' real gifts
and their guilt gifts?

Guilt gifts are nicer.

Why is food better than men?
Because you don't have to wait an hour for seconds.

Why do blokes like smart women?
Because opposites attract.

Why is Santa such a happy bloke?
Because he knows
where all the bad girls live.

Why can't blokes make ice cubes?
They don't know the recipe.

Why is psychoanalysis quicker
for blokes than for women?
When it's time to go back to childhood,
they're already there.

Why do little boys whine?
Because they're practising to be blokes.

Why is Colonel Sanders a typical bloke?
All he cared about was
legs, breasts and thighs.

2 The Dating Game

What's the difference between a circus and a singles bar?
At a circus the clowns don't talk.

Why do men like big breasts and tight pussies?
Because they've got big mouths and small pricks.

What's a man's idea of foreplay?
Half an hour of begging.

What's a bloke's idea of honesty in a relationship?
Telling you his real name.

Why is car insurance cheaper for women?
Because women don't get blow jobs while they're driving.

Why is a computer like a penis?
If you don't apply the right protective measures,
it can spread viruses.

What is a bloke's view
of safe sex?
A padded headboard.

'Do you always use contraception?'
'Yes…'
'Good, so you learned from your parents' mistake.'

Why is a one-night stand like a newsflash?
It's unexpected, brief and
probably a disaster.

*How do you get a man to really
listen to what you say?*
Talk in your sleep.

A bloke and his date were parked on a back road. Things were getting hot and heavy when the girl stopped the bloke. 'I really should have mentioned this earlier, but I'm actually a hooker and I charge £20 for sex,' *she said. The bloke just looked at her for a couple of seconds, but then reluctantly paid her, and they had sex.*

After the cigarette, the bloke just sat in the driver's seat looking out the window. 'Why aren't we going anywhere?' *asked the girl.* 'Well, I should have mentioned this before, but I'm actually a taxi driver, and the fare back to town is £25.*

The Dating Game

How do you know you're in bed
with a blacksmith?
He hammers away and then makes a bolt for the door.

How do you know you're in
bed with a takeaway chef?
You ask for 69 and he gives you egg-fried rice.

How do you know you're in bed with an explorer?
He goes deeper into the bush
than any man has ever been.

How do you know you're in bed with an astronaut?
The equipment is huge, but there's no atmosphere.

How do you know you're in bed with a postman?
He doesn't come when he's supposed to,
and half the time it's in the wrong box.

Chat-Ups & Put-Downs

What do you say to a bloke if he asks
you whether you fancy a quickie?
'As opposed to what?'

What does a girl have to
say to seduce a bloke?

'Hi.'

'I'm an expert in mouth-to-mouth resuscitation – want a demo?'
'I'd have to be completely dead before I let you get that close.'

'Do you like it doggy style?'
'Yes, you can beg all you like, and I'll roll over and play dead.'

'I'd like to get into your pants.'
'I already have one arsehole
in my pants, thanks.'

'We could be having wild sex
by midnight tonight.'

'We probably will be –
but not with each other.'

'Where have you been all my life?'
'Outside your window, in the bushes, with the binoculars.'

'Is that a ladder in your stocking
or a stairway to heaven?'
'You have to be good to go to heaven. Really good.'

'Can I buy you a drink?'
'Can I just have the money?'

'That dress is very becoming on you.'
'But the question is,
would I be coming on you?'

'Are you an optical spanner? Because every time

I look at you I feel my nuts tighten.'

'Lucky you've got nuts because you're not getting a screw.'

'Do you want to come home
and sit on my face?'
'Why, is your nose bigger
than your penis?'

'Word of the day is "legs" – come back to
my place and let's spread the word.'

'Come back when you have enough words
for a whole sentence.'

'*Hey angel, pull up a cloud and sit down.*'
'*Sorry, angels can only talk to people who are dead*
– dead from the neck up doesn't count.'

'*Would you like another drink?*'
'*No, if one doesn't make you look attractive, I don't think two will do the trick.*'

'*Can I give you my number?*'
'*Yes, I'll call you when my dog's on heat.*'

'I'm a magician –
want to see my wand?'

'Can it make you disappear?'

'Your place or mine?'

'Both. You go to yours and I'll go to mine.'

'*I bet you're not a virgin.*'
'**You're right – because not all men are as ugly as you.**'

'*I could make you the happiest
woman in the world.*'
'**You're leaving so soon?**'

'Haven't I seen you somewhere before?'
'Yes, that's why I stopped going there.'

'I wish you were a door –
I could bang you all day.'
'I doubt it; you haven't
got a key that would fit my lock.'

'You've got lovely eyes.'
'Yes, they saw you coming.'

'If your tits were a bit firmer, you wouldn't need that bra.'
'If your cock was a bit firmer, I wouldn't need your brother.'

'If my dog looked like you,
I'd shave its bum and train
it to walk backwards.'

'You should tell your trousers
that it's rude to point.'

'Have you thought of blind dating? Then you'd only frighten them off with your smell.'

'If I throw you a stick, will you leave?'

'I'd love to fuck your brains out, but it looks like someone else got there first.'

'I'd like to leave you with one thought…
It'd be one more than you've had all evening.'

**'If I blindfold my dog,
I might get it to hump your leg.'**

*'You know, you have the body of a god –
Buddha.'*

A bloke is sitting next to a gorgeous woman on a plane. He strikes up a conversation but then she asks if he minds her reading her book.

Bloke: 'No, not at all! What are you reading?'

Woman: 'The Joy of Sex.'

Bloke: 'Hmm. Anything interesting?'

Woman: 'Yeah. Apparently a man's nationality can indicate things about his penis size.'

Bloke: 'OK, like what?'

Woman: 'Well, Polish men have the longest ones and American Indians have the thickest. Oh, by the way, my name is Laura Smith.'

Bloke: 'Nice to meet you, Laura. My name's Tonto Kawalski.'

A bloke is walking through a hotel lobby when he accidentally bumps into a woman and his elbow digs into her breast. 'Oh, sorry,' he says. 'But if your heart is as soft as your breast, I know you'll forgive me.' And the woman replies, 'And if your penis is as hard as your elbow, I'm in Room 103!!'

The blind date didn't go well but as the woman arrives at her door, relieved that the evening is finally over, the bloke suddenly says:

'Do you want to see my underwear?'

Before she can respond, he drops his trousers, right there in the hall, revealing that he isn't wearing any underwear. She glances down and says:

'Nice design – does it also come in men's sizes?'

A bloke and his girlfriend are just about to have sex when she asks if he's got a condom.

'Of course,' the bloke replies. 'In fact I bought a special Olympic pack with gold-, silver- and bronze-coloured ones.' As he starts to put on the gold one, his girlfriend stops him and says: 'Could you put the silver one on?' When the bloke asks why, she replies: 'So you can come second for a change!'

A guy goes into a supermarket and buys a tube of toothpaste, a bottle of Pepsi, a bag of tortilla chips and a frozen pizza. The cute girl at the register looks at him and says: 'Single, huh?' Sarcastically the guy sneers: 'How'd you guess?' She replies: 'Because you're ugly.'

3 *Blokes' Bits*

What's the difference between

a penis and a redundancy cheque?

It's always fun to blow a man's redundancy cheque.

According to women,

pricks come in three sizes:

Small, medium and ohmigod.

According to men,

there are still three sizes:

large,

average

and size-doesn't-matter.

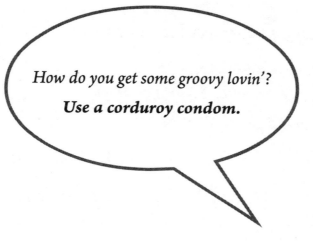

How do you get some groovy lovin'?
Use a corduroy condom.

What do you call a bloke with a small willy?
Justin...

Why do women prefer a circumcised penis?
**Because anything with 10 per cent off
is always attractive.**

Recipe for perfect happiness:

1. A man with a 12-inch penis who can satisfy you all night.

2. A caring man who will do all the housework.

3. A rich man who showers you with presents.

4. Making sure men 1, 2 and 3 never ever meet.

A penis has a sensitive part at one end
– called the glans
– and an insensitive part at the other
– called a **man**.

Heard about the new Viagra eye drops?
They make him look really hard.

A couple meet in a bar and

end up back at his place.

'You don't talk much,'

she says as he's undressing.

'No,' he says,

'I do my talking with this.'

'Sorry,' she says, 'I don't do small talk.'

Man goes into a chemist and asks, 'Do you sell Viagra?'

'Yes,' says the chemist.

'And does it work?'

'Yes,' says the chemist.

'And can you get it over the counter?'

'Yes, if I take two.'

*Why is it dangerous for a man to take Viagra
and iron tablets?*

*Every time he gets an erection
he ends up pointing North.*

What's the difference between an unlucky mouse and a lucky cock?

Nothing – they both end up inside a satisfied pussy.

**Why does a penis
have a big head on the end?**
To stop the man's hand
sliding off and hitting him in the eye.

Two nuns are sitting on a bench

when a streaker runs past.

One has a stroke,

but the other one can't reach.

A man goes into a party shop and says, 'I'd like to hire a costume. I'm going to a fancy dress party as Adam.' So the assistant gets out a fig leaf: 'There you are sir, that's £5.' 'No, that's not big enough,' he says, so she gets out a bigger one. 'That one's £10.' 'Still not big enough,' he says, so she gets out an even bigger one. 'This one's £15,' she says. 'No, I won't fit into that,' he says, so she gets out a hat that says 'Esso'. 'There,' she says, 'wear this, sling it over your shoulder and go as a petrol pump.'

One day Bill noticed that his penis had started growing.

He was delighted as it rapidly reached six inches, eight inches, then ten inches – and so was his wife. By the time it reached 20 inches, however, Bill was finding it difficult to walk, so they went to see a doctor.

The doctor examined Bill and said that he could carry out corrective surgery. Bill's wife looked worried at this. 'But Doctor,' she says, 'How long will Bill be in a wheelchair?'

'Dear lady,' says the doctor, 'Why should he be in a wheelchair?'

'Well, Doctor,' she replies, 'You are going to lengthen his legs, aren't you?'

Men are just like children.

You give them a lovely toy for their birthday
but they're only happy if you let them play
with the box it comes in.

Why is sex like snow?
You never know how many inches
you're going to get
or how long before it turns to slush.

If women had a penis for a day, they would:

1. *Measure it to see whether that really is six inches.*

2. *Pee standing up, without even trying to hit the toilet.*

3. Get a blow job.

4. *Fall asleep without saying thanks.*

5. *Wake up.*

6. *Repeat number 3.*

7. *Repeat number 3.*

8. *Repeat number 3.*

9. *Repeat number 3.*

10. *Repeat number 3.*

What are the ten worst things about being a penis?

1. Your next door neighbour is an arsehole.

2. You can't get excited

without wanting to throw up.

3. Every time you get all relaxed,
someone takes your sleeping bag away.

4. You're bald all your life but with really hairy feet.

5. You've always got two nuts
hanging around you.

6. *Your home is pants.*

7. *In cold weather you shrink.*

8. *You've only got one eye.*

9. *Every time your owner remembers you're there, he tries to strangle you.*

10. *Women would rather see you stiff.*

What's the difference between cinema snacks

and pictures of naked policemen?

One's popcorn and the other's cop porn!

What's the difference between a curtain and an erection?

A curtain doesn't come down

until the performance is finished.

Two brothers are having a medical, and the doctor comments on the unusual length of their penises.

'Yes, sir, we got them from our mother.'

'Your mother? Surely you inherited them from your father?'

'No, sir. You see our mother only has one arm.'

'One arm? What's that got to do with the length of your penises?'

'Well, she had to lift us out of the bath somehow.'

What's the difference between A Midsummer Night's Dream *and* Much Ado about Nothing?

Nine inches is a midsummer night's dream

– three inches is much ado about nothing.

What do you say to an impotent man?
'No hard feelings.'

A girl takes a guy home. When he takes his pants off, he's got the biggest cock she's ever seen – it reaches down past his knees. 'You want a blow job?' she says, but he replies,

'I'd rather fuck. I can do blow jobs myself.'

Why does an elephant have four feet?
Six inches would look silly on an elephant.

What do you get if you cross a penis and a potato?

A dictator.

Who is the most popular guy in the singles bar?
The one in the corner, licking his eyebrows.

'My boyfriend can dial
my telephone number with his tongue.'

'That's nothing. Mine uses his Dictaphone.'

Why do women need blokes?
Because vibrators can't get
a round of drinks in.

Little Johnny is at the zoo with his parents, and he sees the male donkey getting rather excited. 'What's that, Dad?' he asks, pointing to the large thing he can see underneath the donkey. 'Ask your mother, son.' So little Johnny trots over to his mother. 'What's that, Mum?' 'That? That's nothing.' Little Johnny still isn't satisfied so he goes back to his dad. 'Dad, Dad – what is that? Mum said it was nothing.'

'Well, she's been spoilt.'

Blokes' Bits

A man goes to his doctor and says, 'D-d-d-d-doctor, y-you've g-g-got to h-h-h-help me! I c-c-c-can't l-live with this st-st-st-stutter any l-l-l-longer!'

So the doctor examines him and says, 'This is a most unusual case. This stutter is caused by your penis.'

'M-m-m-my p-p-p-penis?'

'Yes, your penis is so long that it's putting strain on the vagus nerve, which is affecting your vocal cords. The only thing I can do is remove half your penis.' Well, the man thinks hard, but eventually he says, 'A-a-all r-r-r-right d-d-d-doctor. I c-c-c-can't st-st-stand the sst-st-stuttering. D-d-d-do it!'

A month later, the same man comes back to see the doctor and says, 'Look, doctor, you've cured my stutter all right, but my wife says sex just isn't the same with a normal-sized penis. On balance, I think I'd rather put up with the stutter. Is there any way the operation can be reversed?' And the doctor replies, 'Nn-n-no, I'm afraid th-th-th-that's n-n-not p-p-p-possible.'

A girl goes up to her boyfriend and says, 'Do you want to hear something that will make you happy and sad at the same time?' 'Go on,' says the boyfriend. 'OK,' says the girl. **'Your dick is much bigger than your brother's.'**

A man is embarrassed about the size of his dick and worried that his latest girlfriend will think it's too small. Eventually he decides to reveal his problem. While they're kissing on the sofa he undoes his zip and guides her hand inside his trousers.

'No thanks,' says the girl. 'I don't smoke.'

Little Lucy tells her friend that her dad has two dicks. 'That's impossible,' says the friend. 'No it's not,' says Lucy. 'I've seen them.' 'So what do they look like?' asks the friend. Lucy says, 'One's small, white and floppy and he uses it for peeing. The other's long, stiff and pink and he uses it for brushing mummy's teeth.'

A man walks into a chemist's owned by a couple of old ladies. 'I have a problem with my penis,' he tells them. 'It's ten inches long and always stays hard, even after having sex for hours at a time. What can you give me for it?' The spinsters whisper to each other. Eventually they come to a decision. One says, 'The best we can offer you is £500 a week and a third interest in the store.'

4 *In The Sack*

In The Sack

When men say, 'Do you have any fantasies?'
they mean, 'Can we try anal sex/you dressing up as
Batgirl/a threesome with your sister?'

When women say, 'Do you have any fantasies?' they
mean, **'I'm so bored that, frankly,**

I'll try anything.'

Bloke says:
'Since I first laid eyes on you, I've wanted
to make love to you really badly.'
Woman replies:
'Well – you succeeded.'

In The Sack

What's the difference between a forged dollar bill
and a skinny man?

One's a phoney buck, the other's a bony fuck.

What's the difference between
a 69 and driving in fog?

When you're driving in fog,
you can't see the arsehole in front of you.

Ten things not to say to a naked man:

1. Is it really that size, or are you standing a long way away?

2. Oh, are we skipping straight to the cigarette?

3. Very funny, now put the real one back on.

4. I hope your tongue is bigger than that.

5. Oh well, no hard feelings.

6. *And what does it want
to be when it grows up?*

7. *You know, maybe we should go fishing instead?*

8. *And your shoes were so huge.*

9. *Still, no danger of a gag reflex tonight.*

10. *Never mind, if we plant it
maybe a great oak will grow.*

Why is sex like a bungee jump?
It's over in no time, and if the rubber breaks,
                              you're in trouble.

What's a bloke's idea of foreplay?
Prodding you to see if you're awake.

Why do women fake orgasm?
Because men fake foreplay.

What's the difference between a clitoris
and a remote control?

A man can put his hand straight
on the remote without looking – every time.

A little girl goes into Santa's Grotto and he asks her what she wants for Christmas.

'I want Barbie and Action Man,' she says. 'Oh,' says Santa, 'I thought Barbie came with Ken.' 'No,' says the little girl, 'Barbie comes with Action Man – she just fakes it with Ken.'

What's the difference between blokes'
sex talk and women's sex talk?

When a bloke talks dirty to a woman,
it's sexual harassment.

When a woman talks dirty to a bloke,
it's £1.60 a minute.

How do you get a man in your bed,
shouting your name and gasping for breath?

Hold a pillow over his face.

What do you call a man with a 12-inch tongue
who can hold his breath for 10 minutes?
Nothing, just keep hold of his ears.

A woman goes into a shop and asks if they sell batteries. 'Yes, we have some in the back room,' says the assistant. 'Come this way.' 'If I could come this way,' says the woman, 'I wouldn't need the batteries.'

In The Sack

Do you know what your arsehole
does when you have an orgasm?
He shouts, 'Hey, what's that buzzing noise
coming from the bathroom?'

John says to his girlfriend,
'Why don't you shout my name out when you come?'
She answers, **'Yeah – like you're ever there when I come!'**

A man walks into a bar and sees a sign 'Win Free Drinks for Life', so he asks the barman how. 'Well,' says the barman, 'You have to pass three challenges. First, you have to drink a bottle of tequila. Next, the landlord's pit bull terrier in the back yard has toothache. You have to go out and pull that tooth. Finally, the landlord's wife is upstairs and she's never had an orgasm. If you can do the business

for her, you get free drinks for life.'
So, the guy thinks he'll give it a try.
He takes the bottle of tequila and
downs it in one go. Then he staggers
out into the back yard. There's
terrible growling and snarling, and
eventually the guy staggers back in,
clawed and scratched all over but
grinning from ear to ear. **'Right,'**
he says, **'that's the first two.
Now where's that lady with
the toothache?'**

Oral sex can make your whole day,
but anal sex can make
your hole weak.

Why is sex like Eastenders?
Just when it starts getting interesting,
it's all over for another night.

In The Sack

Why don't they let male porn stars work at petrol stations?

Because they always pull out the nozzle

at the last minute and spray petrol

all over your windscreen.

If he can't get it up,
you can go down,
but if he can't get it in,
get out.

In The Sack

What three words do men hate to hear during sex?

Is it in?

What three words do women hate to hear during sex?

Honey, I'm home!

A married couple answer the doorbell to find a bald gnome holding a mirror. 'This is a magic mirror,' says the bald gnome. He hangs it on the front door and offers to demonstrate it. Rubbing his head, the gnome says, 'Mirror, mirror, on the door, make me hairy as before.' With a flash, the gnome has a full head of hair. Impressed, the couple buy the mirror, take it into the bedroom and hang it on the bedroom door. First the woman goes up to the mirror, rubs her breasts and says, 'Mirror, mirror, on the door, make my bosoms 44.' There's a flash, and instantly she has 44-inch bosoms. The husband is terribly excited – he rushes over to the mirror, rubbing his cock furiously, and shouts, 'Mirror, mirror, on the door, make my willy touch the floor.' There's a huge flash, and instantly his legs *disappear*.

In The Sack

When God had finished making Adam and Eve, he told them he had two gifts left over. 'First, the gift of being able to pee standing up...' Before he'd even finished, Adam started shouting, 'Oh yes, pee standing up – I'll have that, that'd be brilliant! I'd love that! Please, please, please...'

So God, with an indulgent smile, gives Adam the ability to pee standing up.

'What's the other gift?' asks Eve.

'Oh multiple orgasms...'

'Did you come on the bus, Grandma?'

'Yes, dear, but I passed it off as an asthma attack.'

Little Johnny's maths teacher asks him to define 'average'.

'It's a kind of bed, Miss,' says Johnny.

'A bed?'

'Yes, I overheard my mum saying she has three orgasms a week, on an average.'

A woman walks into the dentist's, takes off her knickers and sits in the chair with a leg over each arm. 'Madam, I think there's been some mistake,' says the dentist. 'The gynaecologist's surgery is on the next floor.' 'No mistake,' replies the woman. **'Yesterday you put in my husband's new dentures. Today I want you to take them out.'**

How many honest, intelligent, attractive, caring men does it take to truly satisfy a woman?
Both of them.

'You never shout my name when you come!'
'No, I don't want to wake you up.'

Why don't women blink during foreplay?

No time.

*45% of women celebrate
National Orgasm Day every year.
The rest just pretend.*

In The Sack

*A*n ambulance is called one Sunday morning to a 99-year-old man who has died in bed. *Amazingly, he appears to have died while making love to his 98-year-old wife.*

'We've always done it on Sunday mornings,' explains his tearful wife, 'because at our age, you have to take it slow. We'd listen to the church bells, ding-dong, ding-dong, in-out, in-out – and we'd still be doing it now, if that damned ice-cream van hadn't turned up.'

In The Sack

*F*or their 50th wedding anniversary, Bill and Sue go back to the cottage where they spent their honeymoon. As they stroll along the country path, Bill says, 'Look, do you remember that tree by the fence?' 'I certainly do,' blushes Sue. 'That's where we had the hottest sex of our honeymoon.' Well, they're both still hot for each other, so they have a look around and, seeing there's nobody in sight, they're soon over by the tree, with Sue leaning against the fence, her skirt hitched up and Bill going at it like a man 50 years younger. In no time, Sue is yelling and thrashing about, and she doesn't stop until Bill is exhausted and has to sit down on the grass. 'I can't have lost my touch,' he says proudly, 'I don't remember you going that wild 50 years ago.' 'Fifty years ago,' says Sue, 'that fence wasn't **electric**.'

What's the difference between sexy and kinky?
Sexy is using a feather.
Kinky is when it's attached to the chicken.

Why is rimming like drinking a Snakebite?
They both leave you shit-faced.

A woman passes a pet shop and sees a sign, 'Clitoris-licking Frog', so she goes in and says, 'I've come about the clitoris-licking frog,' and the assistant answers, 'Oui, Madame?'

Why does a man with a pierced willy make the best husband? He's experienced pain and he knows how to buy jewellery.

Some perverts like to watch a woman wrestle,
but most men prefer to see her box.

What do you get if you cross
a pervert and a hamster?
Letters from
animal rights campaigners.

What's the difference between
an ice cream and a masochist?
An ice cream is often licked
but never beaten...

What do you call a man who's
gagged and tied to the bed?
Trustworthy.

A newly wed couple arrive at their honeymoon hotel, and ask for a double room. 'Since it's your honeymoon,' says the receptionist, 'wouldn't you like the bridal suite?' 'No, it's all right,' says the bridegroom. **'I'll just hold on to her ears till she gets the hang of it.'**

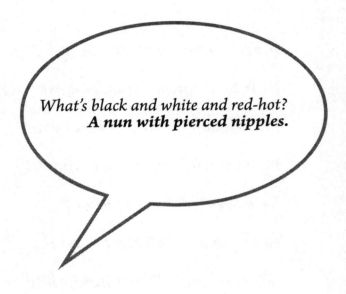

What's black and white and red-hot?
A nun with pierced nipples.

What's the difference between

a masochist and a mosquito?

If you hit a mosquito,

it'll stop eating you.

What kind of sweets do perverts eat?
S&M&Ms

What does a transvestite do at Christmas?
Eat, drink and be Mary.

What's the difference between
a man and a vibrator?

They haven't made a vibrator
that can mow the lawn.

What's the difference between light and hard?

A bloke can sleep with the light on.

What's the difference between your husband and your lover?
About four hours.

How do you make a bloke scream when you are having sex?
Phone him.

A bloke staggers home at 3 a.m. after a pub crawl. On finding his wife awake and naked in bed, he decides to show some interest. He gently kisses her on her forehead but no response. He then softly kisses her lips but still no response. Moving downwards he caresses her neck and then brushes his lips expertly across each breast, before continuing slowly downwards with his tongue until it finds a haven exploring her navel. No reaction whatsoever. His next move is to bend right down and kiss inside her right thigh, just above her knee. At that moment his wife sits bolt upright and screams: 'If it had been a pub, you wouldn't have missed it!'

A woman goes to her doctor for a check-up. The doctor examines her and finds a large lump of pink wax in her navel. 'How did that get there?' he asks. 'Well, it's sort of embarrassing,' says the woman. 'But my boyfriend likes to eat by candlelight…'

A couple are saving up for their holiday, and the husband has the idea of putting some money in a cash box every time they have sex. A month later he counts the money and finds over £800. 'Where did all that come from?' asks the husband. 'I was only putting in £20 a go.'
'You might have been,' replies his wife. 'But not everyone's as stingy as you are!'

Three women were having a laugh, comparing their lovers' techniques in the bed to cars:

The first says, *'My lover's like a Rolls Royce... sophisticated and comfortable.'*

The second says: *'Mine is like a Ferrari... fast and powerful.'*

The third says: *'Well, my lover's like an old Morris Minor... you have to start him by hand and jump on when he gets going.'*

A doctor and his wife have a row about their sex life. It ends with the doctor telling his wife that she's lousy in bed. The doctor goes to work where he calms down and realizes he ought to apologize. He rings home and waits and waits for the phone to be picked up. Eventually his wife answers. 'What took you so long?' asks the doctor. 'Well,' says the wife. 'You know how you said I was lousy in bed?' 'Yes,' says the doctor. The wife replies: **'I was getting a second opinion.'**

5 Rude Tales

A Hell's Angel drops his motorbike off to be mended, and is walking home. On the way he remembers that he's meant to be picking up some things at the hardware shop for the Hell's Angel Clubhouse. 'Ah, yes,' says the shopkeeper, 'Here you are,' and he gets out a bucket, an anvil, a goat, an axe and a black cockerel. 'How am I meant to carry this lot without my bike?' asks the Hell's Angel. 'Well,' says the shopkeeper, 'you could put the cockerel under one arm, the anvil under the other arm, put the axe in the bucket and hold it in one hand, then lead the goat with the other hand.' So the Hell's Angel does as the shopkeeper suggests and starts walking back to the clubhouse. A few yards down the road, he's stopped by a little old lady. 'Excuse me, young man,' she says, 'Can you tell me the way to the chapel?' 'It's right next to our clubhouse,' says the

Hell's Angel, 'so come with me and I'll show you the way. It's just down this alley.' The old lady looks at him very suspiciously. 'Young man,' she says, 'You are a tall, hairy, muscular man and I am a helpless old woman. How do I know you won't get me half way down that alley, push me roughly against the wall, pull down my panties and take me till your wicked desires are sated?' 'Madam,' he replies, 'I have a bucket in one hand with an axe in it, a goat on a string in the other hand, an anvil under one arm and a cockerel under the other arm. How could I possibly push you roughly against any wall?' So the old lady says, 'Put the cockerel down, put the bucket over the cockerel and the anvil on top of the bucket, lay the axe on the ground and I'll hold onto the goat.'

A man walks into a bar with a frog. He puts the frog on the bar and orders a pint and a packet of peanuts. Then he says, 'Billy – catch!' and throws the peanuts to the frog, one at a time, which catches them in its mouth. 'Wow,' says the barmaid, 'a performing frog!' 'Yes,' says the man, 'This frog can do all sorts of tricks. It catches peanuts, it fetches a stick – and it gives the best cunnilingus in the world.'

The barmaid can't believe her ears, so the man says if she doesn't believe him, she can try it for herself. At closing time, the barmaid takes the man and the frog upstairs and lies naked on the bed.

The man puts the frog gently down between her legs but the frog does nothing. 'Billy – cunnilingus!' says the man. Still the frog does nothing. 'Oh, for heavens sake, Billy,' says the man. 'How many times do I have to show you?'

*F*our nuns die and go to Heaven. At the Pearly Gates, Saint Peter stops them.

'Before you enter Heaven, you must be completely pure,' he says. 'Sister Mary, have you ever had the slightest contact with a man's penis?'

'I must confess that I have,' says Sister Mary. 'I once saw a man's penis.'

'Wash your eyes out with this holy water and pass into Heaven,' says Saint Peter.

'Now, Sister Martha, have you ever had the slightest contact with a man's penis?'

'I must confess that I have,' says Sister Martha. 'I once stroked a man's penis with my hand.'

'Wash your hand in this holy water and pass into Heaven,' says Saint Peter. But before he can get any further, the other two nuns have started pushing and shoving.

'Sisters!' says Saint Peter sternly, 'There is room for all in the Kingdom of God. What is the meaning of this unseemly scuffling?'

'If I'm going to have to gargle with that holy water,' says the fourth nun, **'I want to get to it before Sister Catherine sticks her fat arse in it.'**

A woman goes to buy a parrot, and the shopkeeper says, 'We've got one for £100, one for £200 and one for £15.'

'Why is that one so cheap?' asks the woman. 'Well, it used to live in a brothel, so it's a bit foulmouthed.' The woman says she doesn't mind, so she pays her £15 and takes the parrot home.

As soon as she takes the cover off the cage, the parrot says, 'Fuck me, a new brothel!' Then he looks at the woman and says, 'Fuck me, a new Madam.' 'I am not a Madam, and this is not a brothel,' says the woman, but she thinks it's quite funny.

Later on, her two teenage daughters come in. 'Fuck me,' says the parrot, 'new prostitutes!' 'We are not prostitutes,' say the daughters, but they think it's quite funny too. 'Wait till Dad comes in and hears this parrot. He'll go spare.' So they put the parrot in the hall, the door opens and Dad comes in. Dad looks at the parrot, and the parrot looks at him, then the parrot says, 'Fuck me, Dave, haven't seen you for weeks.'

'I don't know what to get my wife for her birthday,' says Bob. 'She already has everything, and she earns more than I do, so she can afford to buy anything she wants.'

'Why don't you give her a voucher saying she can have 60 minutes of great sex, any way she wants?' asks his friend.

'Well, I can't think of anything else,' says Bob, 'so I'll give it a try.'

The next day, Bob's back in the bar. 'I gave her the voucher,' he says. 'Did she like it?' asks his friend. 'Oh yes! She loved it. She kissed me, thanked me for the best present I'd ever given her, and then she ran out of the door shouting, **"I'll be back in an hour!"'**

A young priest *was taking confession in a convent school for the first time.* 'Bless me, Father, for I have sinned,' *says the first schoolgirl.* 'I had impure thoughts about my teacher.' 'Impure thoughts – that's four Hail Marys,' *says the priest.*

'Bless me, Father,' *says the second schoolgirl.* 'I stole a pencil from the stationery cupboard.' 'Stealing – that's six Hail Marys,' *says the priest.*

But the third schoolgirl says, 'Bless me, Father, for I have sinned. I gave my boyfriend **a blow job behind the bike sheds.**' The priest is flummoxed – he's never heard this before, and he doesn't know what penance to impose. Slipping out of the confessional, he meets one of the nuns in the chapel. 'Quick, Sister Lillian,' he whispers. '**What does Father Colin usually give for a blow job?**' '20 quid,' she replies.

A woman fell off her balcony on the 23rd floor, and as she fell, she prayed, 'Oh God, please give me a chance to live!' Suddenly a man leant out from his balcony and caught her in his arms. Before she had a chance to thank him, he asked her, 'Do you suck?' 'Of course not!' she shouted, thinking this can't be what God intended. So the man let go and she fell again, hurtling towards the ground.

Suddenly a second man put out his arms and caught her. 'Do you screw?' he asked. 'No!' she shouted, wondering what the hell God was playing at, sending all these perverts to catch her. So the man dropped her and she continued to fall.

Just as death seemed certain, a third man put out his arms and caught her. Before he could say a word, the woman shouted, 'I suck! I screw!' 'Slut!' cried the man, and dropped her to her death.

A nun is sitting in the bath when there's a knock on the door. 'Who is it?' she says. 'It's the blind man,' comes the reply. So she thinks, that's all right, he won't see me naked and tells him to come in. The man comes in and says 'Blimey, a naked nun. Now where do you want this venetian blind?'

A woman calls a male escort agency and asks for the most mind-blowing sex she's ever had. They say they'll send over their best stud, Ramon. A while later, the doorbell rings but when she answers the door, she sees a man with no arms and no legs down on the floor. 'I am Ramon,' says the man. 'You?' says the woman. 'How can you give me the most mind-blowing sex I've ever had? You've got no arms and no legs.' 'Listen, lady,' says Ramon, 'I rang the doorbell, didn't I?'

A man goes away on a business trip and, as it's a very swanky hotel, his wife comes to join him for the weekend. They have a nice dinner in the restaurant, a drink in the bar, and then they can't wait to go up to their room. In fact, they can't even wait that long – as soon as they get into the lift they're all over each other. The man is pulling her panties down and in less than a minute they're at it. Unfortunately, the doors open at the next floor and the chambermaid gets in. 'Well, really!' says the chambermaid. 'I'm sorry,' says the woman, 'we just had a couple of drinks and got a bit carried away. I don't normally behave this way.' 'I'm sure you don't,' says the chambermaid, 'but this is the fourth time this week I've caught him at it.'

*L*ittle Red Riding Hood is walking through the forest with her basket when out hops a little rabbit. 'Oh, be careful, Little Red Riding Hood,' says the rabbit. 'The Big Bad Wolf is out hunting. If he catches you, he'll pull up your skirt, pull down your panties and shag you!' 'Thanks for the warning,' replies Little Red Riding Hood, 'but I'll be ok.' A little further along the path, a squirrel pops out of a tree. 'Oh, be careful, Little Red Riding Hood,' says the squirrel. 'The Big Bad Wolf is out hunting.

If he catches you, he'll pull up your skirt, pull down your panties and shag you!' 'Thanks for the warning,' replies Little Red Riding Hood, 'but really, I'll be ok.' After half a mile, the Big Bad Wolf jumps out of the bushes and confronts Little Red Riding Hood. 'Now I've caught you,' says the Wolf. 'I'm going to pull up your skirt, pull down your panties and shag you!' Cool as anything, Little Red Riding Hood puts her hand into her basket and pulls out a gun. 'I think not,' she says, pointing her gun right at the Big Bad Wolf. **'I think you're going to eat me, just like it says in the book.'**